The Cree

ERINN BANTING

Weigl

CALGARY
www.weigl.com

Published by Weigl Educational Publishers Limited
6325 10 Street SE
Calgary, Alberta, Canada
T2H 2Z9

Website: www.weigl.com

Library and Archives Canada Cataloguing in Publication Data

Banting, Erinn, 1976-
     Cree / Erinn Banting.
(Canadian Aboriginal art and culture)
Includes index.
ISBN 978-1-55388-339-5 (bound)
ISBN 978-1-55388-340-1 (pbk.)
     1. Cree Indians--Juvenile literature. I. Title. II. Series.
E99.C88B365 2007   j971.2004'97323   C2007-902197-2

Printed in Canada
1 2 3 4 5 6 7 8 9 0 11 10 09 08 07

Project Coordinator Heather Kissock   **Design** Janine Vangool   **Validator** Dr. Robert Innes, University of Saskatchewan

Photograph credits
Every reasonable effort has been made to trace ownership and to obtain permission to reprint copyright material. The publishers would be pleased to have any errors or omissions brought to their attention so that they may be corrected in subsequent printings.

Cover (main): © Canadian Museum of Civilization (III-D-63 a-b, D2004-22740); © **Canadian Museum of Civilization:** pages 14 top (III-D-275, D2004-10541), 14 bottom (III-D-723, D2004-20080), 20 (III-D-63 a-b, D2004-22740), 21 top (V-A-436, D2004-25771), 24 top (V-A-415b, D2004-25523), 24 left (V-A-428 a-b, D-2004-27598), 28 top (V-X-65 h, D2005-07577), 28 middle (III-DD-18, D2003-15584), and 28 bottom (V-A-375, S96-05508); **Department of Indian and Northern Affairs Canada/© Allen Sapp:** page 27; **Glenbow Archives:** page 17 (NA-1851-2).

We acknowledge the financial support of the Government of Canada through the Book Publishing Industry Development Program (BPIDP) for our publishing activities.

Please note
All of the Internet URLs given in the book were valid at the time of publication. However, due to the dynamic nature of the Internet, some addresses may have changed, or sites may have ceased to exist since publication. While the author and publisher regret any inconvenience this may cause readers, no responsibility for any such changes can be accepted by either the author or the publisher.

CONTENTS

The People 4

Cree Homes 6

Cree Communities 8

Cree Clothing 10

Cree Food 12

Tools, Weapons, and Defence 14

Cree Religion 16

Ceremonies and Celebrations 18

Music and Dance 20

Language and Storytelling 22

Cree Art 24

Body Art 26

Modern Artist 27

Studying the Past 28

Timeline 29

Art Activity 30

Further Reading 31

Glossary and Index 32

The People

The Cree are a **First Nations** group that live throughout Quebec, Ontario, Manitoba, Saskatchewan, and Alberta. Historically, they lived in three different regions of what is now Canada. The Woods Cree lived in what is now the northern parts of Saskatchewan and Manitoba, while the Plains Cree lived in the central part of what is now Manitoba, Saskatchewan, and Alberta. The Swampy Cree were found in present-day Manitoba, Ontario, and Quebec.

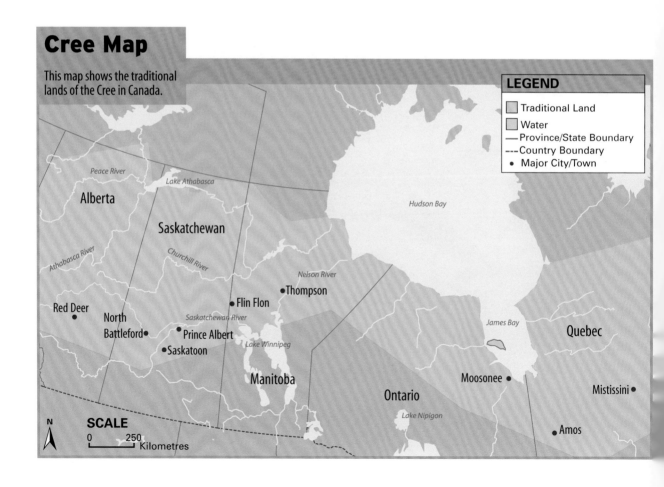

Cree Map

This map shows the traditional lands of the Cree in Canada.

LEGEND
- ☐ Traditional Land
- ☐ Water
- —— Province/State Boundary
- --- Country Boundary
- • Major City/Town

Peace River
Lake Athabasca
Alberta
Saskatchewan
Hudson Bay
Athabasca River
Churchill River
Nelson River
•Thompson
•Flin Flon
Red Deer
North Battleford•
•Prince Albert
Saskatchewan River
•Saskatoon
Lake Winnipeg
James Bay
Quebec
Manitoba
Moosonee •
Ontario
Mistissini •
Lake Nipigon
•Amos

N

SCALE
0   250
Kilometres

MODERN LIVING

The name "Cree" is believed to be a shortened version of the French word "Kristineaux." This is what the French called the Cree when they first encountered them. When European explorers began to arrive in the 1500s, they relied on Aboriginal groups, including the Cree, for information about the land and its resources. English and French explorers began to trade their goods for furs the Cree knew how to access. The Cree became very important to the **fur trade** and the settlement of Canada.

Today, many Cree live on **reserve lands** in parts of Quebec, Ontario, Manitoba, Saskatchewan, and Alberta. They also live in cities and towns across Canada. Many Cree combine their **culture** and **traditions** with their daily life.

The beaver was an important part of the fur trade and is still used by the Cree today. As in the past, beaver skins are stretched onto wooden frames to dry before they are used.

Cree Homes

Depending on the region in which they lived, the Cree had mainly two types of homes. In wooded areas, the Cree lived in birchbark homes called wigwams. On the prairies, the Cree lived in teepees, which were tents covered in bison skin. Both structures were made from wooden frames and were used to shelter their inhabitants from wind, rain, and snow.

Wigwams ranged in size depending on what they were used for. Small wigwams were built as temporary shelters by hunters who followed herds of animals. Larger wigwams were built to house families and were found in Cree villages and settlements.

Teepees were useful to the Plains Cree because they were easily put up and taken down. This was important to the Cree because they moved frequently. As each season passed, they followed herds of bison, caribou, elk, and moose as they **migrated**.

In the winter, the Moose Cree of northern Ontario built homes called shaptwans. They were made out of logs, clay, and peat moss.

DWELLING AND DECORATION

Wigwams and teepees were both constructed with similar materials and in similar ways. First, saplings, or young trees, were cut down and secured in the ground in a circular shape. When building a wigwam, the branches were bent into arches and tied together. Other branches were attached horizontally, to create a strong frame. When building a teepee, the branches were pulled together and tied at the top so their tips stuck out at the end. This was to leave a hole in the top for **ventilation**.

The materials that covered wigwams and teepees were different. Animal skins were normally used to cover a teepee's frame. The skins were warm and waterproof. Wigwams were covered in a variety of materials that formed a thicker and more durable roof and walls around the structure. Bark was most commonly used to build the roof and walls, but animal skins, grasses, and other plants were also used.

Teepees are still used by the Cree during hunting season.

Cree Communities

The Cree have a history of working and living off the land. Community is very important to the Cree because of their tradition of working together for survival.

To follow migrating animals, families travelled together from camp to camp. Once they chose a site, they unpacked their tools and supplies and set up their teepees. Men hunted and fished. Women typically set up camp, prepared food, cared for the children, and made clothing.

There were no rich or poor families in traditional Cree communities. Everyone in the band shared food, clothing, housing, and supplies.

The Cree ruled their communities based on principles of cooperation and respect for the land, their family, their beliefs, traditions, and culture. Cree communities were led by a person, usually a man, called a chief. The chief was usually selected based on his bravery, generosity, and wisdom.

Today, many Cree live in communities with permanent settlements. Advances in

transportation, housing, industry, and modern conveniences have become part of Cree life. Cree living on reserve lands and in other places across Canada still practise the traditions of their **ancestors**, including language, storytelling, music, and art.

Teaching Cree children traditional art forms has helped keep the culture alive.

Today, Cree groups are still ruled by chiefs. These men or women are elected by their communities in the same way leaders are elected throughout Canada. Cree territories are ruled independently of the Canadian government. These communities have their own police forces, governments, and laws.

Mistissini, Quebec, is home to the largest James Bay Cree community. The Cree Nation of Mistissini is run by a council that includes a chief, deputy chief, and several councillors.

Cree Clothing

In the past, the Cree made clothing from fabrics they received through trade and the furs and skins of animals they hunted. Animal hides were warm, waterproof, and lasted for a very long time.

Women wore dresses that had separate sleeves that could be taken off or put on, depending on weather conditions. In warm weather, the sleeves were removed from the dress. In cold weather, the sleeves were added to the garment. The sleeves were attached with string, leather, or twine. Men typically wore leggings and breechcloths. Breechcloths were long pieces of cloth draped over a belt and worn over leggings.

Both men and women wore their hair long, often in braids. The braids were tied with leather strips. Men sometimes wore fur or leather caps decorated with feathers.

Cree women accessorize their traditional clothing with fans, belts, and neck chokers.

When Europeans arrived, they traded with the Cree. The Cree exchanged animal skins for fabric, beads, and metal. They used these materials to add colourful decorations to their traditional clothing. As well, many Cree adopted the European style of dress. They began to wear shirts, blouses, and trousers.

Today, the Cree celebrate their heritage by wearing traditional clothing at special ceremonies and events. Many craftspeople have learned how to make traditional clothing and have passed the art down to younger generations. Cree people today often combine traditional pieces of clothing with jeans or T-shirts.

Cree men had special headgear that was worn at celebrations and during battle. Porcupine hair roaches were headdresses made from the fur of a porcupine. They ranged in style and colour. Some featured the tail of a deer or a feather. The colours used on the hair roach often represented specific religious beliefs. Today, porcupine hair roaches are worn during dances at celebrations and performances.

The Cree often wear their traditional clothing at important ceremonies, including Veterans' Week celebrations.

Cree Food

Like many Aboriginal groups, the Cree relied on the land for all their food. Traditionally, the Cree hunted animals such as caribou, deer, moose, and bison. Cree who lived near water also fished. Birds, such as ducks and geese, were also an important part of the Cree diet.

Animal meat was dried, smoked, or salted to preserve it during the long winter months. The Cree used their dried supplies to make pemmican. Pemmican was made from dried meat, animal fat, and berries or nuts. The mixture was mashed together and dried or stored in containers. People took it on long journeys because it did not spoil.

The Cree also ate nuts, berries, and vegetables. Like meat, the berries were often dried so they could be stored and eaten throughout the winter.

Today, many Cree continue to fish, hunt, and trap animals for food.

Moose Stew

Ingredients

1 kilogram of moose
(or beef) in cubes

29 millilitres salt

1.5 litres water

5 carrots, sliced fine or cubed

1 bundle of celery

500 millilitres of canned tomatoes

2 medium potatoes, cubed

2.5 millilitres savory

1 bay leaf

1 large onion

salt and pepper

cooking oil

Equipment

Large pot

Measuring cups

1. With an adult's help, brown the meat in a large pot. Add the onions, and cook them until they are almost clear.

2. Add the vegetables, spices, and water.

3. Cover, and simmer for at least an hour.

Tools, Weapons, and Defence

Tools were important to the daily life of the Cree. They were often made from materials the Cree had on hand. Wood and rock were collected from the area around their camp. The skins and bones of animals they hunted were also used.

Spoons could be made of wood or bone.

The Cree made knives by sharpening stone. The knives were then used to skin animals and cut food. A large, stone tool called a maul was used to break and split animal bones, which were then used to make tools and weapons. Sacks made from animal skins were used to store food and hold water. Some supplies, such as dried berries, grains, and meat, were stored in containers made from tree bark.

Utensils, such as spoons, were made from the horns of moose, deer, or buffalo. Some Cree also used the shells from shellfish to scoop up their food. Dishes were made from carved wood or birchbark.

The Cree used a tool called a crooked knife to make canoes, paddles, and snowshoes. A rotating movement was applied to the knife to trim, smooth, and even sculpt wood.

HUNTING AND TRAVELLING

Before the arrival of European hunters and trappers, the Cree used bows and arrows for hunting. They also used these weapons during war, along with knives, clubs, and spears.

Bows were made from long pieces of wood. Two sections were cut out on either end to tightly hold the bow strings. Arrows were made by sharpening the end of long, straight branches. Some groups also sharpened arrowheads from rock, bone, or antler and tied them to the ends of long branches. Spears and knives were made in a similar fashion.

Prior to European contact, the Cree depended on dogs and **travois** for transportation. When Europeans arrived, they introduced horses to many First Nations groups. These groups later traded horses to the Cree. These animals greatly transformed the way the Cree lived. Horses represented power and wealth and became an important part of Cree life.

The Cree used snowshoes for winter travel. Caribou hide was laced through the frame to create the webbing.

Cree Religion

The Cree had close relationships with the land where they lived, their families, and their ancestors. Each influenced the Cree's **spiritual** beliefs. The Cree believed that all things in nature should be respected. Animals, places, and people all had spirits, and these spirits helped to guide the living.

Animals that were hunted were very highly respected and honoured. It was customary for the Cree to perform ceremonies to ask for blessings from the animals they hunted. They depended on these animals for food, so these **rituals** were very important. The Cree believed that bad luck came to those who did not respect the spirit world.

The Plains Cree believed that they could see into the future by looking into water. This technique helped them in hunting and war.

Shamans were the religious leaders in Cree society. They were able to communicate with the spirit world and ask for blessings from the spirits. These men or women held special rituals and asked for good fortune for their people. The Cree believed these people had the power to heal the sick and speak to the dead. When a person died, the shaman led special ceremonies that sometimes lasted for days. During the ceremonies, families would join to celebrate the life of the person who had died and share stories about his or her life.

When European missionaries arrived, they encountered symbols of Cree spirituality such as effigies. These monuments often represented animals that were important to the Cree.

The Windigo are Cree spirits. The legend of the Windigo varies from group to group. Some Cree believed the Windigo were evil spirits that tried to harm or curse people. Others believed that Windigo were once people who were captured or bitten by other Windigo.

Most legends tell of a similar creature that hunts humans. Some Cree believe that Windigo only feast on human flesh. Others believe that if a person is bit by a Windigo, he or she becomes a Windigo.

Ceremonies and Celebrations

The Cree held many celebrations and festivals throughout the year. These celebrations honoured family, friends, and nature. They also gave people a chance to give thanks for their good fortune. Celebrations marked important events in people's lives. All celebrations were a time for families and communities to come together and celebrate.

Children usually perform the walking out ceremony by the time they are 2 years old.

One ceremony, called the walking out ceremony, celebrated the time when a child learned to walk. Children were dressed in traditional outfits and given traditional tools and decorations that symbolized the animals hunted by the group. The children were led to a special tent, where a ceremony was held by a shaman or **elder** from the community. Once the ceremony was over, the children and their parents formed a circle around a special tree that was decorated for the ceremony.

When European explorers and traders settled parts of Cree territory, many Cree became **Christians**. Today, the Cree celebrate Christian traditions and holidays such as Easter and Christmas. Some of these celebrations combine Christian traditions with Cree traditions.

Cree communities throughout Canada and in parts of the United States are working to preserve their traditions. Throughout the year, people join to honour their relatives and ancestors and practise the traditions of their elders. Powwows are special celebrations that include dancing, craft making, and storytelling.

GAMES

Games were played for fun throughout the year. Men, women, and children played games of skill and chance. One game played by many Aboriginal groups, including the Cree, was lacrosse. The aim of lacrosse was to score into the other team's goal as often as possible. Each team member held a pole with a net on the end. The net was used to throw the ball. Today, lacrosse is Canada's national summer sport.

Cree powwows often include other First Nations groups of the plains, including the Sioux, Dakota, and Dene.

Music and Dance

Music has always been an important part of Cree life. It was used to celebrate the lives, the landscape, and the history of the Cree people. Traditionally, music was performed at celebrations to give thanks for a happy event or important time of year. In the past, large groups of people would gather to participate.

One of the most important instruments the Cree used in musical performances and celebrations was the drum. Drums were made from birchbark frames and were covered with deerskins. They were pounded with the player's hand or a mallet to make sound.

Some Cree men painted their drums with designs that came from their spirit helper in a dream. These drums could only be beaten on special occasions.

SONGS AND SINGING

Singing was an important part of Cree celebrations. The Cree used songs to thank the spirits for their good fortune. They believed that songs brought blessings and healed the sick.

Songs were performed at celebrations, festivals, and during ceremonies that marked important times in a person's life. Singers usually performed while they danced or for other dancers. Songs were sung by more than one person, and large groups of people often joined in. Cree songs used repeating notes and sounds, and were often accompanied by drums, bells, and rattles.

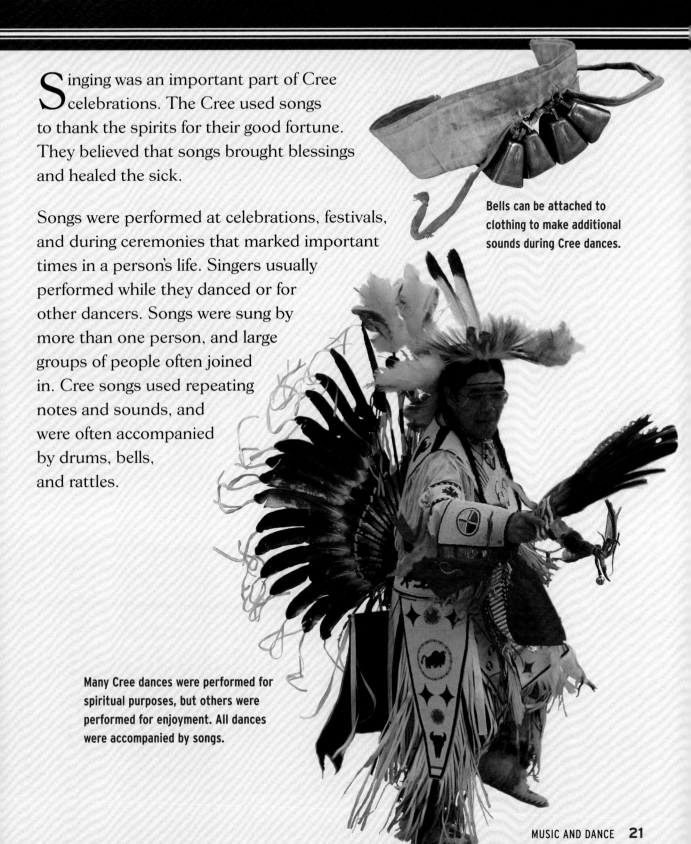

Bells can be attached to clothing to make additional sounds during Cree dances.

Many Cree dances were performed for spiritual purposes, but others were performed for enjoyment. All dances were accompanied by songs.

Language and Storytelling

The Cree speak different **dialects** from the **Algonquian** language family. There are five main dialects spoken by the Cree. These dialects are influenced by the region in which the people live.

The Cree use a special alphabet to write their language. Different symbols are used in different positions to represent the 26 letters of the alphabet. Some **historians** believe the Europeans taught the Cree their written language. Others believe the Cree have used some form of written language for hundreds of years.

Street signs on Cree reserves sometimes feature the Cree language as well as Canada's official languages—French and English.

Even though Cree can be written, it is mainly an oral language that has been passed down from generation to generation through storytelling. Cree stories were told during celebrations, ceremonies, and for fun. They were also used to teach important lessons and the history of the Cree people.

Many of the stories told by the Cree explain their history and origins. One story that is popular with many groups today is how the Cree settled their lands. The James Bay Cree are just one group that has a story of this nature. The James Bay story begins long ago, when the Cree lived a migratory lifestyle and followed herds of animals, with no permanent place to call home. The people lived off the land, hunting and fishing for survival. They were happy, but they wanted a permanent place to live.

One day, the people gathered. One of the elders contacted the Creator to ask for advice. He was told that a goose would be sent to find the Cree a permanent home. The goose flew to all four corners of the continent. Finally, the goose dropped nine feathers around the James Bay area, in present-day Ontario and Quebec. The Cree have lived there ever since.

The Cree language is spoken by more than 45,000 people. Many Cree children in Canada are raised speaking Cree as well as English or French.

Cree Art

The Cree are well known for their beadwork, quilling crafts, and sculptures. Cree artists are inspired by the land around them, the spirits of the animals and people they worship, their history, and their culture.

Beads were often added to clothing and ceremonial outfits. Elaborate and colourful designs and images were sewn together and used to decorate clothing and accessories. Glass beads of different shades and colours were sewn together to depict flowers and geometric shapes.

Cree beading could be found on everyday clothing, including gloves, as well as on more decorative items, such as armbands and hair ornaments.

Cree carvings were created from local materials, such as wood or stone. They often depicted people, animals, or scenes from daily life. Masks were also carved. These were mainly used for celebrations and ceremonies. Masks depicted spirits or animals. They were often worn during musical performances and dances that told stories about the history and culture of the Cree people. The Cree also carved materials used for daily chores, such as knife handles.

Another traditional craft used materials from the Cree people's natural surroundings. The art of birchbark biting is similar to making a paper snowflake. Artists traced a rough pattern on the back of a piece of birchbark and folded the bark into a small square or triangle. The artists then bit the piece of bark in different patterns. The pattern bitten formed an imprint on each of the sections of the folded bark. When it was opened, a geometric pattern emerged.

QUILLING

Before Europeans introduced beads to the Cree people, the Cree used a technique called quilling to decorate their clothing, accessories, and ceremonial items. Quilling, or quill work, was a difficult process. First, the quills of porcupines were soaked and dyed. Soaking the quills made them easier to work with. Dyeing the quills gave them bright colours.

Once they were prepared, the quills were woven into animal skins or bark. Quillwork was used to decorate clothing. It was also used to decorate jewellery, bags, boxes, and baskets. Some items took up to a year to decorate.

Porcupine quills are very difficult to handle. This is why beading became more common among the Cree.

Body Art

The Cree expressed themselves through their art. They decorated their bodies as a way to express themselves, their heritage, and their beliefs.

Face painting was a common practice among the Cree. Animal grease was applied to the skin, and then chalky rock or plant substances were ground and rubbed into the area to create different colours. Red, created with a rock called ochre, was very common. Men also painted their faces during battles.

Tattooing was another traditional form of body art. Tattooing was done as part of a religious ceremony. Both men and women tattooed their bodies, hands, and faces. Tattoos usually consisted of lines and dots. These patterns represented a person's relationships with nature, their family, or their community. Tattooing was done with sharp needles and charcoal.

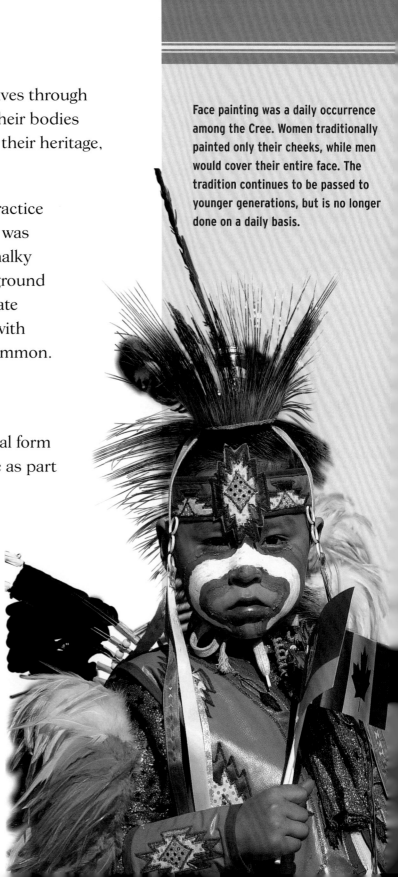

Face painting was a daily occurrence among the Cree. Women traditionally painted only their cheeks, while men would cover their entire face. The tradition continues to be passed to younger generations, but is no longer done on a daily basis.

MODERN ARTIST

Allen Sapp

Allen Sapp was born in 1928. He grew up on the Red Pheasant Reserve in Saskatchewan. When he was born, his mother was sick with a disease called tuberculosis. She did not survive her illness, and Allen was raised by his grandmother.

Allen loved to draw from an early age. Much of his time on the reserve was spent developing his artistic skills.

Over time, Allen decided to move away from the reserve and try to sell his paintings to a larger audience. One day in 1966, Allen decided to take some of his paintings to a medical clinic in his neighbourhood. A doctor there, Allan Gonor, liked his work and bought one of his paintings. He thought that Allen's artwork should reflect his heritage. Allen had painted images he thought people would like instead of images that reflected who he was.

Allen began to paint images depicting scenes from his past and community. He returned to the clinic on a regular basis to

"Sweet Grass Sundance" is just one of Allen Sapp's paintings that captures aspects of Cree life.

show the doctor the paintings he had made.

These new paintings demonstrated the beginning of Allen's unique style. Allen's works, which are made using acrylic paint on canvas, show scenes from daily life for the Cree. The images range from people completing chores to celebrations such as powwows.

Dr. Gonor became one of Allen's greatest supporters. He approached people in the arts community to ask how Allen could find a larger audience for his work. Soon, Allen's works were being exhibited in art

galleries in Canada, Great Britain, and the United States.

Throughout his career, Allen has been celebrated with many awards and honours. Among these honours was his appointment as an Officer of the Order of Canada, which is given to Canadians that contribute to Canadian culture.

Studying the Past

Archaeologists use items from the past to learn about different cultures. **Artifacts** left by the Cree and their ancestors help archaeologists determine what life was like hundreds and thousands of years ago.

Pottery, tools, and the remains of camping sites give archaeologists clues to what life was like for the early Cree. They also provide information on where the Cree settled. Archaeologists have found artifacts in Quebec, Alberta, and Saskatchewan that are thousands of years old. These artifacts also help archaeologists understand the migration of the Cree and their ancestors.

Cree artifacts are displayed at museums throughout Canada. Stone arrowheads, cooking tools, drums, and ceremonial clothing allow people to learn more about Cree culture and traditions.

Cree weapons and musical instruments found by archaeologists help them understand how the Cree lived in the past.

7,000 to 3,000 years ago

Ancestors of the Cree live throughout Canada and the United States. They survive by hunting deer, elk, bear, and beaver. They also fish and collect berries and nuts.

3,000 to 1,000 years ago

The Cree settle in the wooded areas of what are now Ontario and Quebec. They continue to hunt and fish for survival, but also begin to form more permanent settlements. Archaeologists have found pottery from this period.

500 years ago

French explorers arrive in North America in search of furs. They give the name *Cree* to the people they meet.

1670

The Hudson's Bay Company, a fur-trading company, is established in Canada. The Cree are instrumental in its success, which helped to found Canada.

The Hudson's Bay Company is the oldest company in North America. It was founded more than 300 years ago.

1970s

The Cree protest against development in their territory. The Grand Council of Crees is formed to help protect the rights of the Cree people in Canada and parts of the United States.

Make a Birchbark Container

The Cree used materials they found in nature to make tools, clothing, and other items they needed to survive. Bark was used to cover wigwams and to make canoes. Bowls and containers used to hold water were also made from birchbark. In this activity, you can build your own container using bark or construction paper.

Materials

A rectangular piece of birchbark or construction paper

Scissors

Glue

A needle

Wool or thread

1. Fold the piece of paper or bark into a cone shape.

2. Fold the pointed tip up.

3. If you are using paper, glue the cone and tip so that they are secure.

4. If you are using birchbark, have an adult help you sew the seams together.

5. Trim the top of the cone so that it is even.

6. Your container is now ready to be used.

Further Reading

A traditional Cree story is told in *Mwakwa Talks to the Loon: A Cree Story* by Dale Auger (Heritage House Publishing Company Ltd., 2006).

The Cree language is explored in *Cree: Language of the Plains* by Jean Okimasis (Canadian Plains Research, 2005).

Websites

For information on the Cree people and their traditions, visit **www.creeindian.com**.

The history and culture of the James Bay Cree is explained at **www.creeculture.ca**.

To learn the Cree language, go to **www.nisto.com/cree/lesson**.

GLOSSARY

Algonquian: a family of languages spoken by First Nations peoples living mainly in central and eastern North America

ancestors: relatives who lived a very long time ago

archaeologists: scientists who study objects from the past to learn about people who lived long ago

artifacts: items, such as tools, made by human beings in the past

Christians: people who practise a religion based on the teachings of Jesus Christ

culture: the arts, beliefs, habits, and institutions characteristic of a community, people, or country

dialects: variations on a language that is spoken in a certain place

elder: an older and influential member of a group or community

First Nations: members of Canada's Aboriginal community who are not Inuit or Métis

fur trade: the exchange of furs for European goods

historians: people who study the past

migrated: moved from one place to another

reserve lands: lands set apart by the federal government for a special purpose, especially for the use by an Aboriginal group

rituals: systems or forms of ceremonies

spiritual: sacred or religious

traditions: established beliefs, opinions, and customs

travois: a vehicle made of two poles and an attached platform that is pulled by a dog or other animal

ventilation: a means of supplying fresh air

INDEX

archaeologists 28

art 9, 11, 24, 25, 26, 27

ceremonies 11, 16, 17, 18, 19, 21, 23, 24, 25, 26, 28

chiefs 9

clothing 8, 10, 11, 24, 25, 28, 30

food 8, 12, 13, 14, 16

headdress 10, 11

hunting 8, 14, 15, 16, 18, 23, 29

James Bay 9, 23

lacrosse 19

language 9, 22, 23

music 9, 20, 21, 25, 28

pemmican 12

quilling 24, 25

Sapp, Allen 27

shaman 17, 18

storytelling 9, 19, 22, 23

teepee 6, 7

tools 14, 28, 30

weapons 14, 15, 28

wigwam 6, 7, 30

Windigo 17